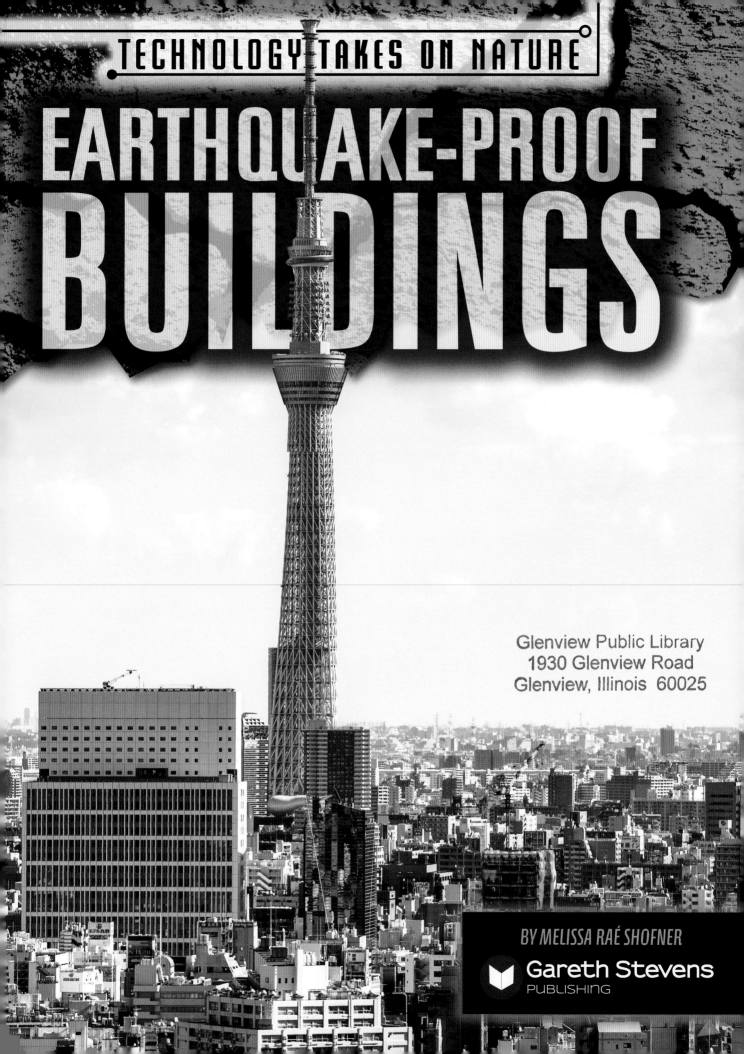

TECHNOLOGY TAKES ON NATURE

EARTHQUAKE-PROOF BUILDINGS

Glenview Public Library
1930 Glenview Road
Glenview, Illinois 60025

BY MELISSA RAÉ SHOFNER

Gareth Stevens
PUBLISHING

Please visit our website, www.garethstevens.com. For a free color catalog of all our high-quality books, call toll free 1-800-542-2595 or fax 1-877-542-2596.

Cataloging-in-Publication Data

Names: Shofner, Melissa Raé.
Title: Earthquake-proof buildings / Melissa Raé Shofner.
Description: New York : Gareth Stevens Publishing, 2017. | Series: Technology takes on nature | Includes index.
Identifiers: ISBN 9781482457674 (pbk.) | ISBN 9781482457698 (library bound) | ISBN 9781482457681 (6 pack)
Subjects: LCSH: Structural engineering–Juvenile literature. | Building–Juvenile literature. | Buildings–Juvenile literature.
Classification: LCC TA634.S56 2018 | DDC 690–dc23

First Edition

Published in 2017 by
Gareth Stevens Publishing
111 East 14th Street, Suite 349
New York, NY 10003

Copyright © 2017 Gareth Stevens Publishing

Designer: Sarah Liddell
Editor: Ryan Nagelhout

Photo credits: Cover, p. 1 Hit1912/Shutterstock.com; background texture used throughout vladm/Shutterstock.com; p. 4 Cantus/Wikimedia Commons; p. 5 BotMultichillT/Wikimedia Commons; p. 6 Spencer Sutton/Getty Images; p. 7 Kevin Schafer/Getty Images; p. 8 Mehmet Cetin/Shutterstock.com; p. 9 Encyclopaedia Britannica/Contributor/ Universal Images Group/Getty Images; p. 11 Pung/Shutterstock.com; p. 12 Vladislav T. Jirousek/Shutterstock.com; p. 13 (main) Sean Pavone/Shutterstock.com; p. 13 (inset) BotMultichill/Wikimedia Commons; p. 15 (main) Junne/ Shutterstock.com; p. 15 (inset) Mangoman88/Wikimedia Commons; p. 17 (main) shinnji/Shutterstock.com; pp. 17 (inset), 21 Koichi Kamoshida/Staff/Getty Images News/Getty Images; p. 18 Paul Sequeira/Getty Images; p. 19 (main) elwynn/Shutterstock.com; p. 19 (inset) A.j.duplessis/Wikimedia Commons; p. 20 Dimas Ardian/Stringer/Getty Images News/Getty Images; p. 23 Bloomberg/Contributor/Getty Images; p. 24 ScoutT7/Wikimedia Commons; p. 25 Arch2all/ Wikimedia Commons; p. 27 Glenn Koenig/Contributor/Los Angeles Times/Getty Images; p. 28 Snek01/ Wikimedia Commons; p. 29 Kennyfoto/Shutterstock.com.

Printed in China

CPSIA compliance information: Batch #CW17GS: For further information contact Gareth Stevens, New York, New York at 1-800-542-2595.

CONTENTS

Words in the glossary appear in **bold** type the first time they are used in the text.

MAJOR DISASTERS

On February 27, 2010, a powerful earthquake shook Chile. An earthquake's power can be measured in magnitude, and this one was magnitude 8.8. More than 500 people were killed, and around 400,000 homes were destroyed. Six weeks earlier, a smaller, magnitude 7.0 earthquake occurred in Haiti. It's believed over 200,000 people died and more than 1 million were left homeless.

The quake in Chile was stronger, but it caused fewer deaths and less **destruction**. That's because Chile's people and buildings were better prepared. Advances in science and **technology** have helped engineers design, or plan out, earthquake-proof buildings in Chile and around the world, keeping people safer when **disaster** strikes.

2010 EARTHQUAKE DAMAGE IN CHILE

THIS STORE IN SAN SIMEON, CALIFORNIA, COLLAPSED, OR FELL DOWN, DURING A MAGNITUDE 6.6 EARTHQUAKE IN DECEMBER 2003. NOTICE THAT THE BUILDING NEXT DOOR IS STILL STANDING.

UP TO CODE

Building codes are rules for designing, constructing, altering, and maintaining buildings in order to keep the people inside safe. There are also special **seismic** codes to make sure buildings are safe during earthquakes. Chile had building codes in place before the 2010 quake hit, but Haiti didn't.

SHAKY GROUND

Earth's crust is made up of pieces called plates. These plates float on a hot layer of molten, or melted, rock and are constantly moving very slowly. The boundaries between the plates are narrow cracks called faults. Earthquakes are a shaking of the ground that occurs along faults when two plates suddenly run into each other or slip past each other.

Three main types of faults exist. A normal fault is when two plates move away from each other. When one plate slides over another, it's called a reverse fault. A strike-slip fault occurs when plates slide by one another in opposite directions.

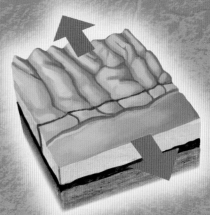

NORMAL FAULT

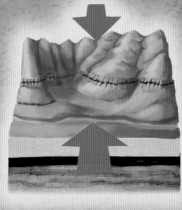

REVERSE FAULT

STRIKE-SLIP FAULT

MEASURING EARTHQUAKES

Scientists once used the Richter scale to measure magnitude, but now they prefer the moment magnitude scale (Mw), which is more exact. The more energy an earthquake releases, or lets go, the higher its number will be on the Mw scale. Powerful quakes cause greater destruction, but earthquake-proofing methods are helping to reduce the **damage**.

SAN ANDREAS FAULT, CALIFORNIA

When two plates slip, stored-up energy is released. The energy vibrates, or moves back and forth quickly, and travels out in all directions. These vibrations are called seismic waves, and there are two kinds. Body waves move deep within Earth. "Primary" means "first," and P waves are the first to be felt. Secondary body waves (S waves) arrive next.

Surface waves, also called Love and Rayleigh waves, travel through the crust and are felt last. They do the most damage to buildings. Deeper quakes cause less damage because they create weaker surface waves.

EARLY ENGINEERS

Mimar Sinan is considered one of the first earthquake engineers. In the 16th century, he reinforced, or strengthened, Hagia Sophia, a religious building in Turkey. Quakes had damaged Hagia Sophia for hundreds of years. Sinan's work still stands today. Earlier still, monuments in ancient Persia were built to resist earthquake damage more than 2,500 years ago!

HAGIA SOPHIA

THESE ENERGY WAVES MOVE OBJECTS IN DIFFERENT WAYS AND CAN CAUSE DIFFERENT KINDS OF DAMAGE TO BUILDINGS.

TYPES OF WAVES

P WAVES
MOVE BACK AND FORTH, CAUSING THE GROUND TO BUCKLE AND BREAK

S WAVES
SHAKE THE GROUND SIDEWAYS AND UP AND DOWN

LOVE WAVES
MOVE FROM SIDE TO SIDE, DAMAGING BUILDING FOUNDATIONS

RAYLEIGH WAVES
MAKE A ROLLING MOVEMENT, LIKE OCEAN WAVES

9

BUILDING A SAFER STRUCTURE

When designing a building in an area with many earthquakes, engineers must pick a construction spot carefully. Structures built on solid rock hold up better than those built on soft soil. Engineers must also review the area's building codes.

Engineers measure the seismic activity of an area before building, too. Earthquakes move the ground in all directions, but buildings aren't commonly built to move at all. Love waves in particular put a lot of horizontal, or sideways, force on a building—suddenly pushing them to one side. Walls, floors, beams, and columns can become stressed, or strained, by this sort of movement. Too much stress can cause great damage to buildings.

THE TRANSAMERICA PYRAMID

The Transamerica Pyramid is one of the tallest buildings in San Francisco at 853 feet (260 m) tall. Several earthquake-proofing methods have been used to help the structure handle the city's frequent quakes. The foundation, or base, of the building is designed to move with an earthquake. The outside walls are also reinforced to allow side-to-side movement.

IN 1989, A MAGNITUDE 6.9 EARTHQUAKE HIT SAN FRANCISCO. THE TOP OF THE TRANSAMERICA PYRAMID SWAYED ALMOST 1 FOOT (30.5 CM) SIDE TO SIDE, BUT THE BUILDING WASN'T DAMAGED.

11

Once engineers know how earthquakes affect an area, they can move on to designing a safe building. Simple structures are better than fancy ones with extra decorations that could break off during a quake. Buildings that are symmetrical, or the same on all sides, often hold up better because they spread out the force of an earthquake evenly over the whole structure.

To handle the strong sideways forces of earthquakes, engineers include several special features in their designs. These include diaphragms, which are a building's floors and roof; trusses, which are **diagonal** structures within a frame; and cross-bracing, which is the use of X-shaped structures that support a frame, among others.

ANCIENT BUILDERS

Peru experiences many strong earthquakes each year, but Machu Picchu still stands today. This is because the Inca, who built the city in the mid-1400s, were excellent builders. They cut stones to fit tightly together, but didn't glue them in place. This allows them to move during a quake and resettle into position afterward.

MACHU PICCHU

PEARL RIVER TOWER

BASE ISOLATION

One popular method of protecting buildings against earthquakes is called base isolation. "Isolate" means "to set apart from," which in this case means separating a building's foundation from the rest of the building. This can be done using bearings, which are parts that allow movement. The bearings are often made of lead wrapped in layers of rubber and steel and are attached, or connected, to the building and its foundation. When an earthquake hits, the foundation can move freely without moving the building above.

Japanese engineers have designed a base isolation system that "floats" a building above its foundation by pushing air between them during a quake!

SHAKE IT UP!

The University of California at San Diego is home to the world's largest outdoor shake table. A shake table is used to test how well a structure will perform during an earthquake. This particular shake table can reproduce the ground movements of major quakes and is big enough to test a 2,000-ton [1,814 mt] structure.

THE UTAH STATE CAPITOL BUILDING WAS BUILT IN 1916. IN 2004, IT WAS FITTED WITH 265 BASE ISOLATORS TO PROTECT THE BUILDING FROM EARTHQUAKES.

ISOLATION BEARING

UTAH STATE CAPITOL BUILDING

15

CORE WALL CONSTRUCTION

An inexpensive earthquake-proofing method is building with concrete reinforced with steel. The "core" of a building is a central, vertical space used for elevators, stairways, and pipes. Walls built around this space are called core walls. Reinforced core walls and base isolation are often used together.

Better still, base isolation can be used with core walls that rock at the ground level. This prevents the concrete from being deformed by earthquakes. To create a rocking core wall, engineers reinforce the bottom levels of a building with steel and run steel cords up the entire building. These cords make the walls more **flexible** so they can handle more stress before breaking.

HIDING FROM THE WAVES

Engineers hope to "hide" buildings from seismic waves using plastic rings. The rings would sit inside each other beneath a building's foundation. Seismic waves would travel through the rings around the building's foundation, exiting on the other side. They wouldn't be able to move up into the building above.

THE TOKYO SKYTREE IS THE SECOND-TALLEST BUILDING IN THE WORLD. IT HAS A CENTRAL CORE CALLED A *SHINBASHIRA* THAT PROTECTS IT AGAINST EARTHQUAKES.

17

SHOCK ABSORBERS

Another widely applied earthquake-proofing method is the use of shock absorbers. These devices absorb, or take in, energy created by bumps and shakes—such as what's experienced during an earthquake—and turn it into heat energy. This heat energy is then dispersed, or spread out, in a liquid. This process is called damping.

When constructing a building, shock absorbers, or dampers, are placed on each floor. A damper is attached between a column and a beam. During an earthquake, the shaking of the building makes the dampers turn the energy of the quake from motion that could cause damage into heat.

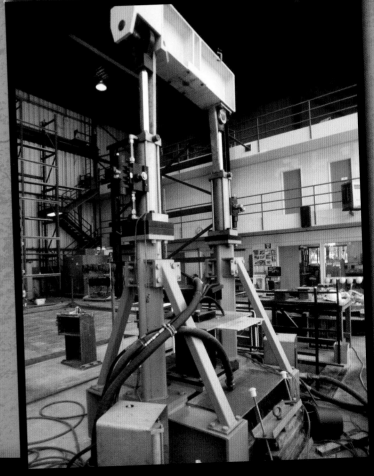

SHOCK-ABSORBING DAMPER

THE TAIPEI 101 BUILDING IN TAIWAN USES THE LARGEST TUNED MASS DAMPER IN THE WORLD. IT WEIGHS 730 TONS (662 MT)!

TAIPEI 101 DAMPER

TUNED MASS DAMPERS

Steel cables support a large mass and dampers near the top of a skyscraper to handle the motions of an earthquake. When a quake occurs, the building sways in one direction as the mass moves in the opposite direction, and the energy is dispersed. These masses, called tuned mass dampers, protect buildings from earthquake damage.

CONTROLLED ROCKING SYSTEM

Engineers are experimenting with a new earthquake-proofing method, called a controlled rocking system, that uses steel frames, cables, and fuses. In a controlled rocking system, the steel frames of a structure are flexible and able to rock on top of the building's foundation. Steel cables hold each frame to the foundation to limit the rocking.

After a quake, the cables can also pull a building back up into position. Steel pieces with metal teeth sit between frames and at the bottom of columns. They work like fuses, absorbing seismic energy as the building rocks. If fuses blow from taking in too much energy, they're easy and inexpensive to fix.

20

SURVIVORS OF A MAGNITUDE 6.3 EARTHQUAKE THAT SHOOK INDONESIA IN 2006 NOW LIVE IN THESE ROUND-SHAPED HOMES. THESE STRUCTURES HAVE BEEN DESIGNED TO ENDURE EARTHQUAKES AND OTHER NATURAL DISASTERS.

A DISASTER-PROOF HOUSE

A company in Japan has designed a small house that looks like a soccer ball. This earthquake-proof structure is called Barier. The 32-sided design spreads out the energy of a quake so the structure isn't damaged. Barier can also float upright, protecting the people inside from deadly **tsunamis**.

SHAPE MEMORY ALLOYS

Concrete and steel are widely used in construction projects. However, earthquakes can greatly damage both **materials**. If the force is strong enough, concrete and steel can be weakened or bent out of shape, which can cause a building to collapse.

Scientists are creating new materials called shape memory alloys. An alloy is a material formed by combining two or more metals, or a metal and a nonmetal. A shape memory alloy can "remember" its original form and return to it, even after experiencing stress. Nitinol is an alloy that's 10 to 30 percent more flexible than steel. Seismic tests show shape memory alloys experience much less damage than more common building materials.

A STICKY SURPRISE

Some Chinese buildings have survived earthquakes for 1,500 years. Scientists discovered they're held together with a superstrong mortar. Mortars are building materials that work like glue to hold pieces of a structure together. They've been in use for a long time. In ancient China, however, their mortar was made using sticky rice!

THIS BUILDING IN JAPAN IS TESTING A FEW EARTHQUAKE-PROOFING TECHNOLOGIES. THE WHOLE STRUCTURE SITS ON RUBBER BEARINGS, AND PART OF THE BUILDING FLOATS ON THE WATER!

23

USING DIFFERENT MATERIALS

One problem with earthquake-proof building technology is that it can be costly. Some countries don't have the money to build safer structures, and as in Haiti in 2010, even smaller quakes can do great damage. Luckily, earthquake engineers understand this problem and are figuring out ways to use inexpensive, easy-to-find materials to construct safer buildings.

Bamboo has been used in India to strengthen concrete. Adobe structures in Peru have been reinforced with plastic mesh, or fine netting. Bearings can also be made using old tires filled with stone or sand. These homemade bearings have been used in Indonesia to help protect houses from earthquake damage.

IN FEBRUARY 2016, A MAGNITUDE 6.4 EARTHQUAKE HIT TAIWAN. THIS SHALLOW QUAKE CAUSED GREAT SURFACE DAMAGE, INCLUDING KNOCKING OVER THIS 17-STORY BUILDING.

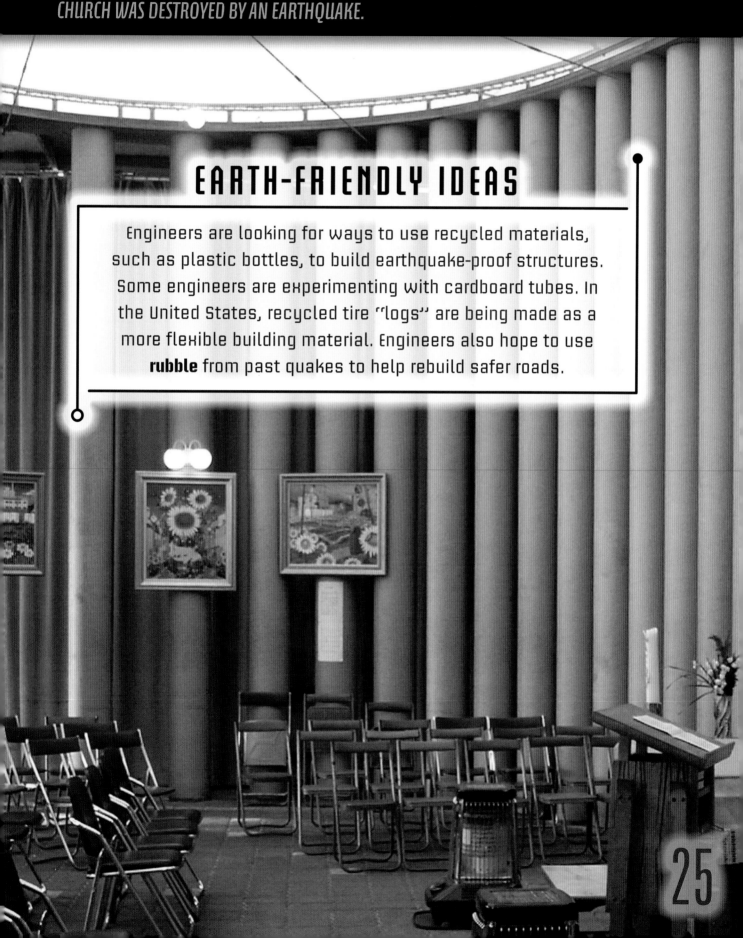

EARTH-FRIENDLY IDEAS

Engineers are looking for ways to use recycled materials, such as plastic bottles, to build earthquake-proof structures. Some engineers are experimenting with cardboard tubes. In the United States, recycled tire "logs" are being made as a more flexible building material. Engineers also hope to use **rubble** from past quakes to help rebuild safer roads.

25

PAST TO PRESENT

New structures are designed and built using the latest technology and building codes. However, it's just as important for older, existing buildings to be **retrofitted** to make them safer during earthquakes. One way this is done is by using fiber-reinforced plastic wrap, or FRP. FRP is a strong, lightweight material that's wrapped around concrete support columns. A filler material is then pumped between the wrap and the concrete. This process can be repeated several times to make a stronger, more flexible column that's wrapped like a mummy!

It's also possible to add base-isolation systems to existing buildings. This is an inexpensive way to protect them from earthquakes.

HUGE IMPROVEMENTS

FRP is used for more than just retrofitting old structures. It's also used to repair support columns in buildings, bridges, and roads that have had structural damage. One study found that weakened support columns beneath a highway that had been fixed using FRP were 24 to 38 percent stronger than unwrapped columns.

IN 2003, PASADENA CITY HALL IN CALIFORNIA HAD A SEISMIC RETROFIT DONE TO PROTECT THE BUILDING FROM FUTURE QUAKE DAMAGE. THE PROJECT INCLUDED ADDING A BASE-ISOLATION SYSTEM.

INTO THE FUTURE

Today, engineers know a lot about designing buildings that can survive the forces of an earthquake. Surprisingly, the future of earthquake-proof building design might actually be found in the animal kingdom.

Scientists are studying byssal threads, which are sticky fibers that mussels use to attach themselves to hard surfaces. Some of these threads are flexible, and others are stiff. Mussels don't wash away in crashing waves because their flexible byssal threads absorb the shock of the wave and spread out the energy. Earthquake engineers are working to create construction materials that act like a mussel's byssal threads.

MUSSEL WITH BYSSAL THREADS

STRONGER THAN STEEL

Spider silk has been shown to be stronger than steel, but what really makes it special is the way it acts under heavy strain. When pulled, a thread of spider silk goes from stiff to stretchy and then becomes stiff again. Engineers hope to copy this quality in future earthquake-proof construction materials.

GLOSSARY

damage: loss or harm done to a person or piece of property

destruction: the state of being destroyed or ruined

diagonal: a straight line that cuts across at an angle

disaster: something that happens suddenly and causes much suffering and loss for many people

flexible: able to move and bend many ways

material: something from which something else can be made

retrofit: to provide a building with new parts that did not exist when it was originally built

rubble: rough, broken stones or bricks used in building

seismic: of, subject to, or caused by an earthquake

technology: the way people do something using tools and the tools they use

tsunami: a great sea wave caused by an earthquake or volcano under or near the ocean

FOR MORE INFORMATION

BOOKS

Salvadori, Mario. *The Art of Construction: Projects and Principles for Beginning Engineers and Architects.* Chicago, IL: Chicago Review Press, 2000.

Graham, Ian. *Megastructures: Tallest, Longest, Biggest, Deepest.* Buffalo, NY: Firefly, 2012.

WEBSITES

Earthquake-Proof Engineering for Skyscrapers
*scientificamerican.com/article/
bring-science-home-earthquake-proof-engineering*
Become an earthquake engineer by building and testing your own structure.

Earthquakes for Kids
earthquake.usgs.gov/learn/kids/
Learn all about earthquakes at this informative website.

INDEX